Banqueting

on the

Bible

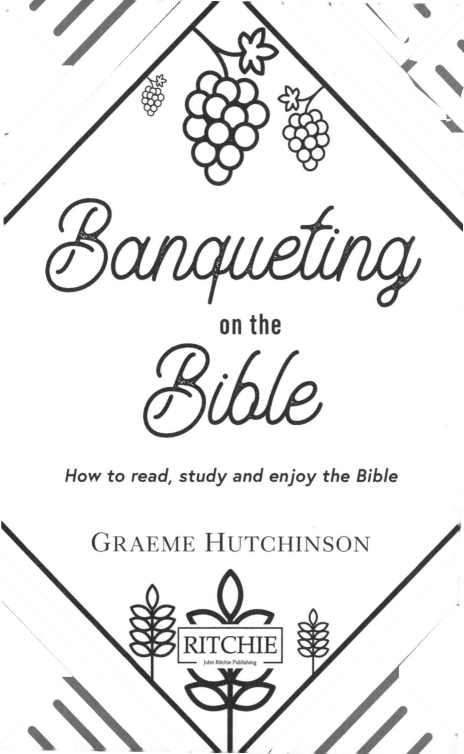

Banqueting

on the

Bible

How to read, study and enjoy the Bible

GRAEME HUTCHINSON

RITCHIE
John Ritchie Publishing

ISBN: **978-1-914273-11-7**

Banqueting on the Bible
Copyright © 2021 by Graeme Hutchinson

Designed by Seventh Visuals UK, Belfast
www.seventhvisualsuk.com

Published by John Ritchie Ltd
40 Beansburn, Kilmarnock, Scotland
www.ritchiechristianmedia.co.uk

Printed by Bell & Bain Ltd, Glasgow

Contents

Foreword

'Thy words were found,
and I did eat them;
and thy word was unto me
the joy and rejoicing of mine heart'
Jeremiah 15.16

How good it would be if these words could be said of each of us! The Bible is to be enjoyed daily, and it certainly provides nourishment for our souls, enriching us with its truths and challenging us to live like Christ.

From the moment the Lord brought Graeme and me together, these words from Jeremiah were 'just Graeme'. On our second date, he brought along his Bible Class notes, sharing his thoughts and studies! This set a pattern for the years to follow. Graeme, who continually feasted on the scriptures, revelled in sharing them, whether we were dandering along country roads or relaxing in the home. His love for the Bible was evident daily.

Apparently this was also seen in his work place. A colleague shared the following with me:

> *'Graeme was a gentleman. It was always clear how much he loved you. Most importantly Graeme was a Christian – something he never hid – his Bible was always on his desk.'*

The same colleague went on to say that she often came on Graeme reading his Bible during the lunch break.

Graeme had a healthy appetite for food, whether savoury or sweet, home-cooked, take-away or fine dining.   He also loved experimenting with new dishes.   Surprisingly, they were always a success – he said all you had to do was follow the recipe! He used to think my traybakes were too small for his appetite.   However, there was no shortage of spiritual nourishment in the Bible and Graeme could concur with the Psalmist in Psalm 119.103:

> 'How sweet are thy words unto my taste!
> yea, sweeter than honey to my mouth!'

When serious illness struck in 2012, the scriptures became even more precious and personal.   We found them to be an inexhaustible blessing as, over the following five years, Graeme and I faced many tough battles.   In those early days when he was hospitalised for long periods, each evening we 'tucked a verse under our tongue' from our daily readings.   That helped us through the night hours until we were together again in the morning.   We would do the same each morning to get us through the day.

Time after time, the Lord provided daily help and encouragement from our regular readings.   We began to mark verses as 'precious promises' or 'very precious promises'.   These afforded strength, comfort, hope and courage, but most of all we experienced the peace of God in those terribly difficult months and years.   During a particularly stressful period when Graeme was at his lowest, the few words he spoke were from the scriptures, evidence that throughout his lifetime he had hidden them in his heart.

Following his home call in 2018, several mentioned how much Graeme's Bible Class at Newtownbreda in Belfast had meant to them, and how they were still using his notes. This has motivated me to share his legacy with a wider audience. What better place to start than the studies from 2008-9, when he sought to urge believers to read, study and enjoy their Bible? He did this by addressing three questions – 'Is the Bible reliable?', 'Is the Bible relevant?' and 'Is the Bible readable?' The Bible was the object of Graeme's research, his spiritual investment and continual delight, because it pointed to the Saviour in whose presence he is now rejoicing.

My prayer is that each reader will be encouraged to find as much delight in God's word as Graeme did, and experience the blessings of the scriptures.

'O taste and see that the LORD is good:
blessed is the man that trusteth in him.'
Psalm 34.8

Avril Hutchinson

Acknowledgements

There are always a number of people involved in bringing a book together and I am particularly grateful to the following for their valuable contribution.

Our nephew Stephen Murdock, for designing the book inside and out. Graeme took a great interest in all his nieces and nephews, and delighted in encouraging them. I know he would be particularly pleased that his nephew has done such a great job on this book.

David Newell, for editing, advising, and keeping me right! Graeme first met David after studying the Church Truths correspondence course, and a firm friendship was established. We both enjoyed David's company each summer in the peace and tranquillity of Donegal and Moneyreagh. As you can imagine, Graeme and David had many profitable discussions on the scriptures.

Family and friends are such a blessing with their love and prayerful support. For all who have encouraged me to keep sharing Graeme – well, here you are!

To all readers who have provided positive feedback and words of appreciation for what has already been shared in various magazines and in the book *The Journey to Jerusalem* (published November 2019) – 'Thank you', because this gives me an incentive to keep on sharing Graeme.

The Bible Class in Newtownbreda over the years gave Graeme a focus for his studies in the scriptures. His teaching encouraged young and old, and I am glad to be able to share his material more widely today.

John Ritchie Ltd, for agreeing to publish another book of Graeme's writings.

Of course, this book wouldn't be possible without an author! I'm so thankful to the Lord for not only blessing Graeme with the ability to teach and write, but also for blessing me with such a husband and very best friend with whom we shared precious years together, creating very special memories.

The Bible

is the greatest of all books;

to study it

is the noblest of all pursuits;

to understand it,

the highest of all goals.

Charles C Ryrie

in the Introduction to *The Ryrie Study Bible*

Introduction 1

'God's sacred Word among us;
which is that inestimable treasure,
which excelleth all the riches of the earth'

(Preface to Authorized King James Version)

2011 marked the 400th anniversary of the publication of the Authorized King James version of the Bible. This book is designed to provide some factual truths about the Bible – the believer's most treasured possession.

IMPORTANCE

The human word is important and powerful (James 3.4-6), but the word of God is more so (Heb 4.12). The Bible is the bedrock of the Christian faith. Consider its

Revelation: Humans are made in the image of God to have fellowship with Him (Gen 1.26). God is revealed in His creation (Psa 19.1-4) but, in a special way, through the scriptures (Psa 19.7-11).

Documentation: God communicates verbally (Heb 1.1), but the record needs to be preserved (Exo 17.14). The Bible is God's written record and is *progressive* (with two testaments); *personal* (revealing the Son of God) and *panoramic* (extending from eternity past to eternity future).

Compilation: The Bible was written over a period of around 1,500 years with approximately 40 different writers, but this mode of revelation has now ended. *The Canon is closed.* From as early as the second century, the 66 books of the Bible formed the written and final record of God's revelation (1 Cor 13.8-12). We are not to add to the revelation (Deut 4.2; Prov 30.6; Rev 22.18-19). *The Scriptures are sufficient:* 'it is a sufficient guide for **every** aspect of Christian belief and practice' (Brian Edwards, *Nothing but the Truth*, Evangelical Press, 2006, p 192).

Preservation: God committed the original Old Testament text to the Jews, who ensured its protection as the oracles of God (Rom 3.2). The original text of the New Testament completes the word of God. It is the subject of hatred and ridicule (Gen 3.1), but it cannot be destroyed (read Jeremiah 36.21-32 in light of Psalm 119.89).

Edification: Personal experience teaches that the Bible is necessary to feed the soul of the believer and promote growth and development (1 Pet 2.2).

INSPIRATION

The Bible is what it claims to be – the word of God (1 Thess 2.13). Consider the following:

Meaning: Every time we read the Bible (or verses/passages are quoted in our hearing) it is as though God Himself is speaking the words. The key text is 2 Timothy 3.16: 'All Scripture is God-inspired' (AV, Newberry margin). The Bible records the words that 'proceedeth out of the mouth of God' (Matt 4.4). The entire text of scripture, in its original Old Testament and New Testament language, has literally been breathed out by God.

Method: Peter explains the approach taken to document the written word of God (2 Pet 1.20-21). The term 'moved' by the Holy Spirit is important – elsewhere in the New Testament it refers to a ship being carried along by the wind (Acts 27.15,17). The writers of scripture were under the control of (or carried along by) the Holy Spirit, and wrote what God wanted them to write.

Misunderstandings: Number 1 – Were the writers of scripture human keyboards, used by the Holy Spirit to transcribe the word of God? No! The word of God retains the distinctive personality of the individual human writers. The style of each of the four Gospels is one such example. Number 2 – Were the writers given the broad thrust of the message but had scope to add their own details? No! The word of God is the word of God. The *words* of scripture are themselves God-breathed (1 Cor 2.13).

Message: The central theme of scripture is the Lord Jesus and hence large portions of the Bible are prophetic in nature (Rev 19.10). This predictive quality, and its subsequent fulfilment, makes the message of the Bible unique in nature and divine in origin. 'Without divine inspiration, prophecy is so risky a business that the so-called sacred books of human religions contain practically nothing of it' (Rene Pache, *The Inspiration and Authority of Scripture*, Moody, 1969, p 282). The Bible, however, is sourced in God, who knows the future and directs the course of history.

INERRANCY

The *Chambers English Dictionary* defines inerrancy as 'freedom from error': a succinct and accurate description of the Bible.

Logical: The scriptures are the word of God; He is unable to lie (Titus 1.2); therefore the Bible is free from error.

Total: Each word of the original text of scripture is God-breathed, so each word is inerrant (though it may accurately record error and lies, for example, Genesis 3.4). This is true of doctrine, ethics, geography, history, and every subject of scripture (Prov 30.5).

Practical: The continual reading of the 'word of truth' (John 17.17) is the only basis by which the Christian can live holily in an unholy world.

INTERPRETATION

In studying the word of God, there are a number of principles of interpretation:

No 1 – Literal: 'If the literal sense makes common sense then seek no other sense lest it result in nonsense!' This principle assumes that, as God wants His revelation to be understood, we need to apply the normal rules of communication: look to the plain sense of what has been written (and do not seek for double meanings).

No 2 – Dispensational: Because God administers the affairs of His creation in various stages, we need to understand their differences as we interpret scripture. For further detail consult *Dispensationalism* by Charles Ryrie (Moody Publishers, reprint 2007).

No 3 – Contextual: We must look to the immediate context (historical, cultural, and geographical) to interpret properly the meaning of scripture. 'A text without context is a pretext!'

No 4 – Devotional: Bible study is to inform the mind and inflame the heart, so we need to look for the Saviour in our daily reading of scripture (Luke 24.27).

No 5 – Methodical: Haphazard and slothful approaches to Bible study will yield poor results. Secular books (such as novels) are read from cover to cover and so too must scripture.

ILLUMINATION

Illumination is the means by which God takes the words of scripture and applies them to the heart.

Author: The Holy Spirit resides within the believer to reveal the truth of scripture (John 16.13). If we grieve or quench the Holy Spirit (Eph 4.30; 1 Thess 5.19), we shall fail in our Bible study.

Blessing: The Bible sheds light on the need of salvation and how/where it can be obtained (Rom 10.17; 2 Tim 3.15). The believer's pathway is also illuminated by the word (Psa 119.105), and prayer is a vital component of Bible study (Acts 6.4).

Christians: Fellow believers are to help each other with their understanding of scripture (Acts 18.26). Believers in the early church were marked by fellowship around the truths of scripture (Acts 2.42).

In the beginning

was the *Word,*

and the *Word* was with God,

and the *Word* was God.

John 1:1

The Saviour and the Scriptures 2

'Learning from the Master'

(Brian Edwards, *Nothing but the Truth*, Evangelical Press, 2006, p 144)

The Saviour's appreciation and utilisation of scripture is a lesson for believers today to follow in His steps.   In the context of the Bible, consider the following facts.

PROFOUND IN ITS MINISTRY

The Bible is 'not like any other book' (*Interpreting the Bible*, Peter Masters, Wakeman Trust, 2004), not least because of its association with the Saviour.

Spotlight on Christ: The Lord taught that the scriptures spoke of Him (Luke 24.27; John 5.39, 46-47).   The three sections of the Old Testament (the Law, Prophets and Psalms) all bear witness to Christ (Luke 24.44).

Similarities with Christ: The Lord is the incarnate Word (John 1.1; Rev 19.13), whereas the Bible is the inspired word (2 Tim 3.16).

Both communicate the truth of God, with vital links to the Spirit (Luke 1.35; 2 Pet 1.21). However, the Saviour is the object of worship while the scriptures are a pointer to Him.

Sanctification to Christ: The Lord spoke of the scripture's power to sanctify the believer (John 17.17). Conformity to the Saviour is dependent on conformity to the Bible.

POWERFUL IN ITS AUTHORITY

The Saviour's use of scripture confirmed it to be fully authoritative. For the evidence, consider the points below:

Author: The Saviour highlighted the 'God-breathed' character of scripture during His temptations (Matt 4.4). As the Son of God, His words were as authoritative as God's Word (Matt 24.34-35).

Blessing: The Saviour outlined the importance of the Bible to salvation (Luke 8.11,15; 10.25-26). His enemies' failure to recognise His credentials as Messiah was attributed to their ignorance of the truth (Matt 22.29).

Completeness: Miracles had their place in His earthly ministry, but the Saviour confirmed the absolute sufficiency of scripture (Luke 16.31). In the workplace, we are encouraged to 'think outside the box', but, when it comes to preparation for eternity, we err when we 'think outside the Bible'!

Durability: In John 10.34-35 the Saviour deployed a Psalm (Psa 82.6) not only to refute the charge of blasphemy but also confirm His 100% confidence in the abiding truth of scripture: it [the scripture] cannot be voided or annulled.

Effectiveness: The Saviour used the scripture as a weapon to defeat the devil (Matt 4.1-11). He did the same when He interacted with the religious leaders (Matt 12.3,5; 19.4; 21.42; 22.31).

PRECISE IN ITS HISTORY

The Saviour considered the Old Testament to consist of real people and events. Most importantly, it constitutes the source of instruction for the child of God.

Far-reaching: In Luke 11.51 the Saviour displayed His complete grasp of scripture – the murders of Abel and Zacharias are the first and last recorded in the Hebrew Old Testament (Chronicles being the last book).

Factual: The Saviour confirmed many Old Testament passages that continue to be ridiculed by the enemy: the accounts of Adam and Eve (Matt 19.4-6); the flood in the days of Noah (Matt 24.37-39); the experiences of Jonah (Matt 12.40); and the prophecy of Daniel (Matt 24.15).

Functional: The Saviour used scripture for spiritual and practical purposes (over and above the confirmation of history). For example, Adam and Eve support the life-long institution of marriage (Matt 19.4-6); the serpent of brass points to the work of Calvary (John 3.14), and the manna anticipates the provision of Christ to satisfy the soul (John 6.31-51). Bible study should fill both head and heart.

PINPOINT IN ITS ACCURACY

The Saviour came to fulfil Old Testament scripture, insisting that its reliability extended to the smallest detail (Matt 5.17-18; Luke 16.17).

Essential: As the Lord Jesus is the subject of prophecy (Rev 19.10), the Old Testament scriptures which anticipate Him have been (and will be) fulfilled.   Relative to the volume of prophecy, only a few portions remain to be fulfilled.

Exact: For example, in His birth the Saviour fulfilled scripture (Matt 1.22-23; 2.5-6,15,17-18,23), as He did in His death (Matt 26.24,31,54-56; 27.35,46; John 19.24,28,36-37) and resurrection (1 Cor 15.4).

Encouraging: The biblical account of the Saviour's earthly sojourn is a powerful witness to its inspiration and inerrancy.

PRACTICAL IN ITS TESTIMONY

The Saviour's adherence to scripture carries important practical teaching for present-day Christian witness.

Proclamation: The Saviour was clear and authoritative in His reading of scripture (Luke 4.16-22).   We too should be able to read the Bible aloud and without mumbling.

Quotation: The Saviour knew the scriptures and routinely quoted from them (and not from other sources, such as the Apocrypha). This was true in both hard times (for example, Luke 23.46 and Psalm 31.5) and good times (for example, Luke 24.44-45).

Submission: In His fulfilment of scripture, the Saviour (as the perfect Servant) taught the importance of abiding by its instruction (Hebrews 10.5-7 is a key text but also consider, for example, Luke 18.31).

Meditation: Throughout His ministry, the Saviour displayed the importance of literally interpreting (Old Testament) scripture, but He also savoured its truth (Isa 50.4).

Illumination: The Saviour confirmed the importance of the indwelling Holy Spirit. The Spirit of truth is the divine guide who enables the believer to understand divine truth revealed in the word (John 14.17; 16.13).

Satisfaction: Periods of Bible study with the Saviour left His audience encouraged and strengthened (Luke 24.32). Like the two on the way to Emmaus, may we know what it is to have spiritual (and scriptural) heartburn!

Open thou mine eyes, that I may behold wondrous things out of thy law.

Psalm 119:18

The Psalmist and the Scriptures 3

'This sacred ode is a little Bible, the Scriptures condensed'

(Charles H Spurgeon, *The Treasury of David, Volume 3,* on Psalm 119, Hendrickson, p 131)

In understanding the importance of the Bible for believers today, it is useful to recognise its value to those who lived in an earlier generation. Consider the Psalmist and Psalm 119.

SOURCE OF SCRIPTURE

The Psalmist is clear on the divine origin of scripture (see verses 1,72,115). For the Psalmist, the Bible is:

Authoritative: The truth of God's word is essential for daily living. The scriptures contain ordinances and precepts that must be obeyed (for example, vv 91,93).

Accurate: Because they are divine in origin, the Psalmist confirms the inerrancy of the scriptures (vv 30,43,140,142,151,160). Verse

160 shows that the Psalmist believed the sum of the scriptures to be truth.

Ageless: The eternal nature of scripture was a particular delight (v 89). Divine truth cannot perish or decay as it abides in heaven.

Assorted: The introductory names used to describe the scriptures – law (v 1), testimonies (v 2), ways (v 3), precepts (v 4), statutes (v 5), commandments (v 6), judgments (v 7), word (v 9) – all point to its varied teaching. The Bible contains history and prophecy, births and deaths, poetry and prose, and much else besides.

Accessible: The Psalmist wrote about the scriptures because he was able to read them. When it comes to knowing God (v 66), we are not left to imagination – He has revealed Himself in His word.

STRUCTURE OF SCRIPTURE

The Psalm reflects a general characteristic of scripture. It is **not** a collection of haphazard sayings but a structured unfolding of One who is Himself marked by order (1 Cor 14.33).

Dimensions: Psalm 119, the longest Psalm, is the only one 100% absorbed with teaching on the scriptures. Today we have the complete canon, but is our appreciation of the word as deep as that of the Psalmist?

Divisions: Psalm 119 is an alphabetical poem, composed of twenty-two sections each containing eight verses. The opening line of each section starts with a letter of the Hebrew alphabet and continues until all twenty-two letters are used. Thus the structure is not easily forgotten (see v 61).

Details: Each section can be studied independently of the rest. Consider the last section (vv 169-176). Here we learn that *perception* comes alone from God (v 169); *prayer* and the scriptures go together (v 170); *praise* will be richer as we read the word (v 171); *proclamation* of the truth is our responsibility (v 172); *precepts* are found in the word (v 173); *pleasure* is derived from reading scripture (v 174); *protection* ('help' meaning aid or succour) comes from God's judgments (v 175); and the word has *power* to restore us to the divine Shepherd (v 176).

STUDY OF SCRIPTURE

The Psalmist is a 'role-model' as we seek to grasp divine truth. Like him, we need to understand the following:

Affection: The Psalmist had a deep and abiding love for God's word. There are repeated references to 'love', with the more prominent expressions found in verse 97 and verse 167.

Blessing: The first word of the Psalm, 'blessed' (compare Psalm 1 and Psalm 32), reveals a person who knew, from experience, the inner joy that comes from meditating on the word (vv 1-2).

Commitment: The Psalmist was not an irregular reader, dipping into scripture now and again. 'Night and Day' the scriptures were before him (read verse 148, then verse 97).

Duty: Time and again the Psalmist reminds the Lord that his desire was not only to read scripture but also to keep its truths (see, for example, verse 2). Furthermore, the scriptures were a treasure-chest (v 162) of endless joy and enrichment.

Enlightenment: Divine truth requires divine revelation (John the Baptist was conscious of this, John 1.32-33). The Psalmist regularly asked Jehovah to reveal nuggets of truth (for example, consider verses 26-27). Divine wisdom, when imparted to the believer through the

Bible, is the best form of education (vv 98-99).

Fascination: When reading the scriptures, the Psalmist maintained a sense of awe (vv 18,161). We too must retain a sense of excitement as we turn to the Bible.

Goodness: The word of God brings wholesome goodness to the reader (v 66), not least because the God of the word is good (v 68)!

Heart: Students of scripture must be 'whole-hearted' in their reading (vv 2,10); 'clean-hearted' in their worship and walk (vv 7,9,11); and 'open or large-hearted' as they absorb the precepts from the Lord (v 32).

STRENGTH OF SCRIPTURE

A key word in the Psalm is 'quicken', which means to enliven or revive (compare Hebrews 4.12). Consider, for example, how the scriptures have power to promote

Faithfulness: The Psalmist's desire was to remain true to God and His word (vv 25,37,107).

Righteousness: The inerrant word is the only source of morality and truth for believers who live in a godless world (vv 40,50,156).

Lovingkindness: Since God is love, the believer should read the scriptures in order to display the same attribute (vv 88,159).

SATISFACTION OF SCRIPTURE

The complete Psalm is a testimony to the blessing of scripture.

Memorability: The poetry of the Psalm ensures that it, and scriptures generally, are kept in remembrance (vv 16,52,93,109).

Meditation: The Psalmist regularly refers to his habit of pausing to reflect on the teaching of scripture (for example, verse 15). This is pertinent ministry for the action-fuelled world of the 21st century.

Manifestation: The Psalm reflects a general principle, namely that the Bible reveals the character of God (vv 7,68,75,90,114,119,137,151).

Ministry: The word is uniquely able to stimulate joy (vv 111,162), peace (v 165), longsuffering (vv 28,75), goodness (vv 39,66) and faith (v 42).

Metaphors: The Psalm contains a well-known metaphor for scripture – a lamp/light (v 105).   May its truth be our daily guide.

THE ENGLISH ALPHABET & PSALM 119
A selection of words and themes in Psalm 119 to encourage further study

A	author	vv1, 115
	affliction	vv50, 67, 71, 75, 92, 107, 153
	awe	vv18, 27, 129, 161
B	blessing	vv1, 2
C	comfort	vv50, 52, 76
	cleansing	v9
D	desire	vv20, 40, 131
	direction	vv105, 133
E	enlightenment	vv18, 27, 34, 66, 73, 104, 125, 130, 144, 169
	emotion	vv53, 136, 158
	eternal	vv89, 142, 144, 152, 160
F	fear	vv38, 39, 63, 74, 79, 120
	faithful	vv86, 90, 138
G	guidance	vv24, 105, 170
	goodness	vv39, 66, 68

ℋ	help	vv86, 173, 175
	heart	vv2, 7, 10, 11, 32, 34, 36, 58, 69, 70, 80, 111, 112, 145, 161
	holiness	vv11, 101
	hope	vv43, 49, 74, 81, 114, 116, 147, 166
ℐ	illumination	v105
	inerrancy	vv30, 43, 140, 142, 151, 160
𝒥	joy	vv14, 16, 24, 35, 47, 70, 77, 92, 97, 111, 143, 162, 174
	judgment	vv84, 126, 137
𝒦	keep	vv2, 4, 5, 8, 17, 22, 33, 34, 44, 55, 56, 57, 60, 63, 67, 69, 88, 100, 101, 106, 115, 129, 134, 136, 145, 146, 158, 167, 168
	knowledge	vv66, 75, 79, 125, 152
ℒ	love	vv47, 48, 97, 113, 119, 127, 132, 140, 159, 163, 165, 167
	lamp/light	vv105, 130
ℳ	meditation	vv15, 23, 48, 78, 97, 99, 148
	mercy	vv41, 58, 64, 76, 77, 124, 132, 156
	mouth	vv13, 43, 72, 88, 103, 108, 131, 171, 172

N	nearness	v151, 169
	night	vv55, 62, 148
O	ordinances	v91
	obedience	vv9, 21, 51, 87, 91, 102
P	peace	v165
	persecution	vv42, 51, 61, 69, 78, 85, 86, 87, 95, 110, 157, 161
	praise	vv7, 164, 171, 175
	prayer	v170
	protection	vv114, 117
Q	quickening	vv25, 28, 37, 40, 50, 88, 93, 107, 149, 154, 156, 159
R	remembrance	vv16, 49, 52, 55, 61, 83, 93, 109, 141, 153, 176
	respect	vv6, 15, 117
	righteousness	vv7, 40, 62, 75, 106, 123, 128, 137, 138, 142, 144, 160, 164, 172
S	salvation	vv41, 81, 123, 155, 166, 174
	search	vv2, 10, 45, 94, 155
	scope	v96
	song	v54
	sweetness	v103

T	teach	vv7, 12, 26, 33, 64, 66, 68, 71, 73, 108, 124, 135
	trust	v42
	treasure	vv14, 72, 162
U	unchanging	vv89, 142, 144
	upheld	v116, 117
V	value	vv72, 127
W	walk	vv1, 3, 32, 45, 59
	witness	vv13, 27, 46
	wonderful	vv18, 27, 129
	wisdom	vv98, 99
X	x-ray	v11
Y	youth	v9
Z	zeal	vv131, 139

God,

who at sundry times
and in divers manners
spake in time past unto the fathers

by the prophets.

Hebrews 1:1

The Prophets and the Scriptures 4

'The Spirit of God worked within and through their [the prophets'] own personalities to reveal His truth'

(Robert L Saucy, 'Scripture – Its Power, Authority and Relevance', in *Understanding Christian Theology*, C Swindoll and R Zuck, Nelson, 2003, p 32)

What can we learn from the Old Testament prophets' appreciation of the scriptures?

REVELATION: THE DIVINE WORD

Old Testament prophets were divinely appointed to foretell the future and forth-tell the word of God (Ezek 1.1-3). Their teachings were **God-given:** Through a variety of approaches (appearances, dreams, visions, miracles, etc) God spoke to His people via the prophets (Heb 1.1). A large section of the Old Testament represents the written record of these revelations.

Spirit-sent: The Spirit of God was instrumental in using the Old Testament prophets to record the revelations (Zech 7.12; 2 Pet 1.20-21). The same is true for the New Testament apostles (2 Pet 3.2).

Christ-centred: A large portion of Old Testament prophecy relates to the character and coming of Messiah (John 1.45). We should read Old Testament scripture with that in mind.

INSPIRATION: THE LIVING WORD

A pivotal Old Testament passage which teaches that the scriptures are the inspired word of God is Isaiah 55 (vv 10-11). Consider the following:

Analogy: The hydrologic cycle can be traced to scripture! A key observation is the parallel between the rain and snow descending from heaven, and the word coming from Jehovah's 'mouth' (Deut 8.3).

Application: The cycle of blessing, evident in creation, is also evident in the Bible. Rain and snow have a pre-determined purpose and so too have the scriptures. They descend from heaven, revealing the need and source of salvation, but they also educate the believer to praise God (the cycle of blessing returns to heaven).

Assurance: Four times in one verse the reader is reminded of the power of scripture to accomplish the divine will (repetition of 'shall' in Isaiah 55.11). Hebrews 4.12 is one New Testament passage which focuses on the same truth.

DOCUMENTATION: THE WRITTEN WORD

Aside from oral communication, the prophets recorded the word of God in written form (Exo 24.3-4; Isa 30.8; Jer 30.1-2).

Note the following:

Purpose: In each and every generation (Deut 31.24-29) the written word provides a fixed reference point for God's people. The scriptures outline the will of God for His people.

Proximity: The commandments of the Old Testament were provided in a format that ensured they were within reach (Deut 30.11-14). The scriptures are heavenly in origin but God, in grace, has ensured their accessibility on earth.

SEGMENTATION: THE ORDERED WORD

The Old Testament scriptures follow an orderly progression but there is an important paradox to note.

Diversity: Each of the thirty-nine books of the Old Testament falls within three sections: history, poetry, or prophecy. With this division, God ensures that His word caters for our need, irrespective of how we feel.

Unity: No part of the Old Testament is unrelated to the Messiah (Luke 24.44). He is the cord that binds scripture together. 'The Christian has one Bible, not two; worships one God, not two; knows one way of salvation, not two' (J Blanchard, *How to enjoy your Bible*, Evangelical Press, 2007, p 43).

MEDITATION: THE APPLIED WORD

The scriptures were a central part of David's life, not least when he performed the dual role of king and prophet (Acts 2.30). Read Deuteronomy 17.14,18-20 in conjunction with Psalm 19.7-11.

Learn the Word: Kings were instructed to 'write', 'read' and 'learn' the scriptures (Deut 17). David later testified (Psa 19) to the reliability of scripture as 'perfect', 'sure', 'right', 'pure', 'clean', 'for ever', 'true' and 'righteous'.

Live the Word: Kings were to 'keep' the law and the statutes, and 'do them' (Deut 17). David experienced 'great reward' from keeping the scriptures (Psa 19.11).

Love the Word: In terms of their value, the scriptures are worth more than gold. In their consumption, they are sweeter than honey and the honeycomb (Psa 19.10). Do we value the scriptures in this way and apply them to our daily walk?

PROCLAMATION: THE SPOKEN WORD

God spoke directly to His prophets (Isa 8.5; Jer 36.2; Ezek 3.10). Furthermore, aside from documenting the truth, they were also charged with proclaiming it to others (Isa 20.2; Jer 37.2; Ezek 38.17). Although there are no prophets today, we are still charged to proclaim the word to others (1 Thess 2.13).

PRESERVATION: THE ETERNAL WORD

Jeremiah 36 is an important passage teaching the indestructibility of scripture. Four realities are evident:

Inspiration: The prophecies of Jeremiah were not home-made but heaven-sent (vv 1-2). Previously the prophet had been instructed that the divine word was akin to a fire and hammer (Jer 23.29) – now he witnessed the reality of these symbols.

Proclamation: Though barred from the temple, Jeremiah instructed Baruch to proclaim the word of God before the people (vv 6,8,10,15).

Opposition: In conveying divine truth, the scriptures present teachings that make sinners uncomfortable and troubled (for example, King Jehoiakim, vv 22-23).

Preservation: In response to the destruction of the word, Jeremiah was instructed to rewrite the scriptures (with Baruch acting as his amanuensis, vv 27-32). 'Man can burn a scroll, but he cannot destroy the Word of God' ('Jeremiah', Charles H Dyer in *The Bible Knowledge Commentary (Old Testament)*, Victor Books, 1986, p 1181).

EDIFICATION: THE NOURISHING WORD

Jeremiah and Ezekiel both testified to the nourishing power of the word (Jer 15.16; Ezek 2.9-3.4). Note the following:

Consumption: The staple diet of Old Testament prophets was the word of God. Jeremiah fed on the scriptures ('fed' indicates consumption – note the first Old Testament reference in Genesis 2.16). 'We must go to Scripture as a thirsty man goes to a well; as a hungry man goes to a meal' (C H Mackintosh, *Short Papers on Scripture Subjects*, Believers Bookshelf, 1995 reprint, p 5).

Application: Charged with a solemn message (Ezek 2.10), Ezekiel first consumed the truth before proclaiming it to others (Ezek 3.1, 4-7). Likewise, we must first study scripture, understanding its truth, before we seek to proclaim it to others.

Satisfaction: Both prophets were satisfied with the scriptures. Jeremiah was burdened (Jer 15.10), particularly at the response of the people to the scriptures (Jer 8.9), but he rejoiced in the word (Jer 15.16). Ezekiel, like the Psalmist (Psa 19.10), found the scriptures to be sweet and satisfying (Ezek 3.3).

If any man speak,
let him speak as the

1 Peter 4:11

The Apostles and the Scriptures 5

'The apostles have provided us with an insight into a deeper or fuller meaning of the Old Testament'

(Brian Edwards, *Nothing but the Truth*, Evangelical Press, 2006, p 165)

Having sought to outline the attitude of the Old Testament prophets to the scriptures, we now turn to the New Testament apostles and consider Paul's view of scripture as outlined in the epistle to the Romans.

THE SCRIPTURES: UNIQUE

The dictionary's definition of 'unique' is 'having no like or equal'. This summarises the attitude of Paul to the word of God.

Authorship: In Romans 3.2 Paul referred to scripture as 'the oracles of God' (see also Acts 7.38; Heb 5.12; 1 Pet 4.11). They represent the very words of God (with their truth initially committed to the nation of Israel – see Rom 9.4; Psa 147.19-20).   The prophets (Hosea is cited as one example, Rom 9.25) were used to record God's written word (Rom 15.4).

Accuracy: The apostle refers to the Bible as 'the holy scriptures' (Rom 1.2).   This description confirms that Paul considered the Bible to be sacred, pure and without error (2 Tim 3.15).

Authority: Paul considered the scriptures to be fully authoritative in all aspects.   For example: *theology*, there is one God over both Jew and Gentile (Rom 3.29); *ministry*, only faith in the work of God can bring salvation (Rom 4.3); and *history*, Paul refers to a range of Old Testament characters as genuine historic figures (for example, Adam and Moses in Romans 5.14).

THE SCRIPTURES: UNDERSTANDABLE

The epistle confirms that the Bible can be accessed by any of God's children.

Revelation: The scriptures stand as bookends to the epistle (Rom 1.2; 16.26) and both references teach that God delights to reveal Himself to His people.   This revelation is *personal* (about Himself, His Son, and the Holy Spirit – Rom 1.1-4) and *progressive* (the mystery of Jews and Gentiles being united through the gospel was a secret only revealed in the New Testament – Rom 16.25-26).

Quotation: The apostle uses over fifty quotations from the Old Testament.   Two points emerge from this statistic.   Firstly, we can and should seek to memorise scripture.   Secondly, what the Bible says, God says.   For example, in Romans 7.7 Paul states that the law condemns covetousness (the Old Testament reference is from Exodus 20 where God is the direct speaker); in Romans 9.17 Paul refers to scripture speaking to Pharaoh (the Old Testament reference is from Exodus 9.13-16 where God is the speaker).

Interpretation: Paul uses various Old Testament characters to press home important truths. For example, Abraham and David illustrate the principle of trust (Rom 4); Adam is contrasted with the Lord Jesus (Rom 5); Isaac and Jacob show God's prerogative to save whomsoever He will (Rom 9); and Elijah/7,000 unnamed believers teach that God is faithful to those who serve Him (Rom 11).

Consolation: The written word of God is designed to comfort the people of God (Rom 15.4). In times of worry we should resort to the word.

THE SCRIPTURES: USABLE

Within each section of the epistle the apostle displays how the word of God can be applied to every avenue of life. For example:

Sin: In the opening three chapters the apostle shows that both Jew and Gentile are sinners before God. In proving the reality of sin (Rom 3.9-18) Paul draws on a range of scriptures – five from the Psalms and one from the Prophets (Isaiah).

Salvation: Between Romans 3.21 and Romans 5, the plan to save guilty sinners is outlined. We learn that salvation upholds the righteousness of God and justifies those who believe on His Son. The role of the Old Testament is to bear testimony to the saving grace of God (note the reference to 'the law and the prophets' in Romans 3.21).

Sanctification: In the section between Romans 6 and the end of Romans 8, Paul shows that salvation brings us into a new association with Christ: freedom from the law and life through the Holy Spirit.

There are references from the Law (Rom 7.7; Exo 20.17) and the Psalms (Rom 8.36; Psa 44.22), the latter teaching that nothing, even extreme persecution, can separate the believer from Christ.

Sovereignty: The gospel enables the believer (Jew or Gentile) to access the same spiritual blessing. Furthermore, between Romans 9 and Romans 11 the apostle teaches that God **will** fulfil His Old Testament promises to Israel. A variety of Old Testament references are used, with the central chapter teaching some sublime truth regarding scripture (for example, Romans 10.17).

Service: The concluding section (Rom 12-16) gives practical guidance on Christian living. From responsibilities to the assembly and government (Rom 12-13) to personal conduct and evangelism (Rom 14-15), the scriptures are used to outline our duty as believers (for example, Romans 12.20; 13.9).

THE SCRIPTURES: UNCHANGEABLE

One chapter of the epistle (Rom 15) can be used to confirm the eternal character of God's word.

The Sections of Scripture: In the chapter, the apostle draws from the three sections of the Old Testament to support his teaching – the Law (v 10), the Psalms (v 3) and the Prophets (v 12). This consistency (between Old and New Testament) confirms that scripture is immutable.

The Strength of Scripture: The phrase 'it is written' is repeated throughout the chapter (for example, verses 3,9,21). It confirms the durability of the word; it cannot be broken (Jer 23.29; John 10.35). 'The phrase ['it is written'] is significant in that it registers the fact that what follows is part of the written and unbreakable word of God'

(B Edwards, *Nothing but the Truth*, Evangelical Press, 2006, p 160).

The Subject of Scripture: The chapter confirms that the Lord is the theme of the Bible – He is the One who accomplished the will of God despite the cost (v 3), and He established Old Testament truth through His ministry (v 8). Both the incarnate Word and inspired word are immutable.

THE SCRIPTURES: UP-TO-DATE

The epistle displays the dual truth of Bible history (for example, Romans 5.14) and prophecy (for example, Romans 11.25-27). If the record of the past is shown to be accurate (which it has been), we should be confident about what the Bible says regarding the future.

Man shall not live
by bread alone,
but by every

word

of

God.

Luke 4:4

Weapon to Defend God's Truth 6

> *'He [the Lord] was not tested with a view to ascertaining whether He would fail, but rather to prove to those of a doubtful mind that He could not fail'*

(Lewis Sperry Chafer, *Systematic Theology*, *Vols 5&6*, Kregel, 1993 reprint, p 84)

The scriptures are important for every aspect of Christian living, not least when we are engaged in battle. Consider how the Saviour used the scriptures when He was victorious over the devil.

ADVERSARY

The New Testament passages documenting the temptation of Christ illustrate, in part, the Satanic opposition to the word of God (Matt 4.1-11; Mark 1.12-13; Luke 4.1-13). Consider the following:

His Title: The enemy of the truth is aptly described as 'the devil' (Matt 4.1,5,8,11). The title captures the aim of Satan to accuse falsely or to slander (Rev 12.10).

His Tactics: The devil seeks to cast doubt on the word of God (compare Matthew 3.17 with 4.3,6). He has honed his approach ever since Adam and Eve dwelt in the Garden of Eden (Gen 3.1). He has a knowledge of the Bible but endeavours to misuse and contradict its truth (compare Matthew 4.6 with Psalm 91.11-12).

His Timing: It was immediately after His baptism that the Lord faced the temptations (Matt 3.16-4.1). We learn an important principle, namely that periods of blessing are often followed by warfare.

His Testing: It was, of course, impossible for the Lord to fail as there was nothing within Him to respond to the devil (John 14.30). The temptations (meaning to try) are recorded to prove that the Lord was not able to sin.

BATTLEGROUND

Since believers often lurch from battle to battle, there follow some important principles from the Lord's temptation. Note, for example, that the trial is:

Inspired: The Spirit led the Saviour into the wilderness (Matt 4.1). For us, it is clear that when we allow God to lead, the resulting experiences are God-given and are designed to develop our faith.

Intense: Everything associated with the temptations was real and severe – the devil, the wilderness, and the duration of 40 days/ nights. A summary is found in Hebrews 2.18: 'He himself hath suffered being tempted'.

Irregular: The recorded trials came in a threefold cycle. In Matthew 4.3-4 the strategy was to induce *sustenance without the scriptures*; in Matthew 4.5-7 it was *shelter without submission*; and in Matthew 4.8-10 it was *success without suffering*. The devil can switch his attack (2 Cor 11.14-15; 1 Pet 5.8) and we need to be on guard.

Important: This experience enables the Lord to sympathise with our trials (Heb 4.15 – though as the impeccable Saviour He remains sinless and unique). He knows what it is to face the rigorous onslaught of the devil; but He equally knows how we can be triumphant.

COMFORT

The Lord overcame the devil with a resource available to every child of God – the scriptures. Consider their

Source: In His exchange with the devil, the Lord confirmed the divine origin and authority of scripture (Matt 4.4).

Style: In the record of the temptations, the individual style of each Gospel is retained. Matthew emphasises the royal credentials of the Saviour (Matt 2.2; 27.37); his account of the temptation concludes with a reminder that the kingdom will come from God (not the devil). Mark presents the Saviour as the perfect Servant; with the focus on His service there is only a brief account of the temptation (Mark 1.12-13 – but note the description of 'wild beasts'). Luke portrays the Saviour as the perfect Man (a common title in the Gospel is 'Son of Man'). His account of the temptation is preceded by the genealogy of the Saviour, traced back to Adam (Luke 3.38). The pattern is also different from Matthew. Luke emphasises the sequence we face (1 John 2.16): the lust of the flesh (Luke 4.3-4), the lust of the eyes (Luke 4.5-8), and the pride of life (Luke 4.9-13).

Subject: The incident outlines a compact summary of the Bible. Divine truth is presented; the devil is shown as the enemy of truth; the Saviour is confirmed as the bodily display of divine truth; victory can only be secured through the Lord Jesus.

Sufficiency: Notice that it was enough for the Lord to quote from the Bible. There is sufficient power in the word to defeat whatever enemy we encounter.

DEPLOYMENT

A major lesson from the passage is in the use of scripture. As an aide-mémoire, consider the following questions:

What? Identifying the enemy (their location and strength) is half the battle. Unlike the Saviour, our enemy is threefold: the devil, the world (Rom 12.2) and the flesh (Rom 7.18). Submission to the word of God and using it in battle will bring victory.

Why? Access to the same weapon (the scriptures) ensures that every believer is not left vulnerable in battle. We have nothing to take pride in, but rejoice in the power of God's word.

When? Similar to Gideon (and other Bible characters), we use the scriptures at all times and particularly in the heat of battle (Jud 7.14,18,20,22).

How? The Lord responded to the temptations by quoting scriptures. Warfare is not a time for sermons but the heart-felt application of a God-given resource.

Where? Note that the Lord was tempted in the wilderness (Matt 4.1, meaning desolate and solitary). As pilgrims in the wilderness (1 Pet 2.11), we can only gain victory over the devil by **using** the scriptures; hence we must continually read and meditate on the word. It is, therefore, important to have in our possession a Bible that displays the evidence of usage. Remember, as someone has said, 'A Bible that is falling apart will normally be owned by a believer who isn't!'

Who? Only the believer can truly discern the power of the word (1 Cor 2.14). Others may ridicule, but the word of God is a vital resource for the spiritual soldier.

EFFICACY

The temptations of the Lord prove His impeccable character and the power of God's word.

Symbol: The scriptures are likened to a sword (Eph 6.17), a small sword for fighting at close quarters. It has a unique power to overcome the enemy (Heb 4.12).

Spirit: Only the Spirit-filled believer can effectively use the scriptures (Eph 5.18; 6.17). It is therefore incumbent on the believer to combine holy living with the daily and systematic reading of the scriptures.

Swordsman: The Lord's experience in the wilderness is a pattern in using the right scripture in the right way and at the right time. As ever, we ought to 'follow his steps' (1 Pet 2.21) in order to gain victory over the enemy (1 Cor 15.57).

Walk circumspectly ...

Redeeming the time ...

Understanding what the

will of the Lord is ...

Be filled with the Spirit.

Ephesians 5:15-18

Roadmap to Discern God's Will 7

'There is nothing higher for man than to find and do the will of God'

(Lewis Sperry Chafer, *Systematic Theology, Vols 7&8*, Kregel, 1993 reprint, p 309)

The scriptures, which reveal the will of God, are the primary resource for believers to understand their daily responsibilities. The following points seek to provide 'five words' of understanding (1 Cor 14.19) on this important subject.

A WORD OF CLARIFICATION

What do we mean by the will of God? From Acts 16, consider some of the different aspects.

God's predetermined will: The sovereign will of God is unchangeable as Ephesians 1.11 states 'In whom also we have obtained an inheritance, being predestinated according to the purpose of him who worketh all things after the counsel of his own will'.

God's prescribed will: Prior to the ascension, the Lord revealed His will for the spread of the gospel (Acts 1.8). The enemy challenged the message, but the pattern was unchangeable. The blueprint can be traced in the following passages: Acts 5.28 (Jerusalem); 8.1 (Judea); 8.5 (Samaria); and 16.9-10 (uttermost part of the earth, with Philippi as the start of the spread into Europe). The mandate for gospel preaching in Philippi (and elsewhere) goes back to the scriptures and, in particular, Matthew 28.19-20. However, the believer is called to do much more than preach the word. Standards for Christian living, assembly gathering, and other issues are also outlined in the Bible – the authoritative and unchanging source for believers to discern the will of God (Eph 5.17; 1 Thess 4.3; 5.18; 1 Pet 2.13-15). The Christian must read the scriptures in order to know and do the will of God (Col 1.9).

God's permissive will: In the accomplishment of His sovereign will the Lord often permits the believer to engage in certain actions. One example is found in Acts 16.7 where the missionaries tried to enter a certain area (Bithynia) but were prevented by the Holy Spirit. Remember that the steps (and stops) of a good man are ordered by the Lord (Psa 37.23).

A WORD OF COUNSEL

How can we discern the will of God? Acts 16 provides some important principles, with a phrase in verse 10 being of particular significance: 'assuredly gathering' – literally meaning to knit or piece as one, indicating that the points below should be taken in conjunction with each other.

Talk to the people of God: As part of the second missionary journey (Acts 15.36 – 18.22) Paul decided that Timothy, instead of Mark, should be his companion. Why? Acts 16.1-3 indicates the favourable report that Christians from Derbe and Lystra gave of Timothy – Paul had evidently obtained their views (see also Acts 15.40 with regard to Silas). We too should seek counsel from other believers as we endeavour to discern the will of God (Prov 19.20; 24.6).

Test the mind of God: As indicated previously, the team of missionaries attempted to enter Bithynia with the gospel but were prevented by the Holy Spirit (Acts 16.7). Neither Paul nor his companions were criticised for trying the door! God often reveals His will by means of the closed door.

Trace the Spirit of God: Notice the fervency by which the servants in Acts 16 were dependent on the Holy Spirit (Acts 16.6-7) – they were evidently led by the Spirit (Gal 5.18).

Trust the Son of God: Emphasis on the divine will is given at both the start and end of the second missionary journey (see Acts 16.1-10 and Acts 18.21). Being Spirit-filled, the believers were pointing toward the subject of the gospel – the Lord Jesus (John 16.13-14).

Thrive on the Word of God: Read through the account of the second missionary journey and note the priority given to the scriptures (for example, Acts 16.32; 17.2,11,13; 18.11). In particular, observe the systematic approach of the apostle to his Bible preaching and teaching. The same ought to apply to our daily reading schedule. It has been said that we do not find God's will from the Bible by opening it at random. Rather, we are to study all the scriptures so that every word may instruct us.

A WORD OF CAUTION

Although God, in His sovereignty, can use the events of life to guide His children, we must not place over-reliance on circumstances. For example, the New Testament believer is called to walk by faith and not by sight (2 Cor 5.7). This means precisely what it says! Our life on earth should be marked by trust – not in ourselves but in God and His word (Psa 119.105). Furthermore, it is evident that circumstances are often misleading. David may have thought God's will was that he should slay Saul (1 Sam 24.1-7). Jonah may have interpreted the ship to Tarshish (and the means to pay) as proof that he was allowed to pursue a particular path (Jonah 1.1-3). However, on both occasions the apparent circumstances were contrary to the mind and will of God.

A WORD OF CHALLENGE

In Acts 16 the teaching on the scriptures and the will of God can be summarised as follows:

Discerning God's will: It was, of course, important for Paul and his companions to 'know' where they were to serve. But remember that the guidance only occupies ten verses (Acts 16.1-10) of a lengthy chapter.

Doing God's will: The larger section of the chapter is devoted to describing how the servants discharged God's will, preaching to and teaching the converts in Philippi. Are we active in doing what we know to be the will of God?

Delighting in God's will: The servants also delighted in God's will, even when it proved costly (Acts 16.22-25). The implications of this truth are immense. We can only fulfil our joy by doing God's will rather than our own.

A WORD OF COMFORT

It is unsurprising to note that the scriptures are clear in teaching that God's work (Deut 32.4), way (Psa 18.30) and will (Rom 12.2) are all 'perfect'. This should be of immense comfort to the child of God when it comes to knowing and doing the will of God.

Blessed

are they which do hunger
and thirst after righteousness:

for they shall be *filled*.

Matthew 5:6

Food to Develop God's Children 8

*'Milk is crucial to the growth of any
baby and God's Word is crucial to the
growth of the new Christian'*

(John MacArthur, *Why Believe the Bible?*, Regal, 2007, p 120)

Christians have a responsibility to grow (1 Pet 2.2; 2 Pet 3.18) and
the scriptures provide a staple, varied and full diet. In 1 Peter 1.22
to 2.3, consider how this growth can be nurtured.

REACH OUT!

Because Christians are a target for attack (1 Pet 5.8), it is therefore
important for us to work together in mutual support. In our primary
passage, Peter outlines some important principles of Christian love.

Foundation: Far from being empty or sentimental, Christian love
is founded on 'truth' (receiving the gospel as taught in scripture –
1.22). Part and parcel of the Christian diet is the combination of
love and truth (1 Cor 13.6).

Features: The standards for Christian love are high (1.22). It must be genuine rather than pretend, stemming from a clean heart and marked by fervency.

Focus: Peter speaks of 'love of the brethren' (see also chapter 3 verse 8). Top of our daily 'to do' list must be love for fellow believers which, in itself, promotes individual and corporate growth.

Flows: The references to 'divine love' in the epistle are worth a study (1.8; 1.22; 2.17; 3.10). The order in the first chapter is important: love for the Saviour is our priority, but it should then flow out to one another. Note the 'one another' ministry of the epistle (1.22; 4.9; 5.5,14).

THINK BACK!

Peter asks his readers to reflect on their salvation (1.23 – having been 'born again'). Remembering 'what I am' should influence 'what I do' (activity) and 'what I want' (ambition).

Birth: Salvation is both a second birth ('again' – 1 Peter 1.3) and spiritual birth ('from above' – John 3.3). To produce Christian *fruit* (loving fellow believers), Peter considers the *root*, the new birth which gives us a supernatural capacity to love (Rom 5.5).

Bible: Instrumental to the believer's salvation and development is the word of God (1.23-25a). The passage reminds us that the scriptures are vital for growth (just as seed is to plants) and are incorruptible, presenting absolute truth (a key attribute of God, 1.4,18-19). They also have a divine origin (1.23) and are therefore immutable (impossible to change) and durable (unlike the grass and flowers of the field - Isa 40.6-8).

Blessing: The Bible contains the 'gospel'; that which the believer has received (1.25b) and which angels desire to comprehend (1.12).

LAY ASIDE!

As with any diet, believers need to refrain from certain things (2.1), and work to satisfy their appetite with the scriptures and the Saviour (2.2-3).

Terminology: We are exhorted to 'lay aside' those things that are inconsistent with our new nature. It is worthwhile reading other verses in the New Testament where similar phrases are found (Rom 13.12; Eph 4.22,25; Col 3.8; Heb 12.1; James 1.21). 'Peter's words picture someone flinging off a badly stained or infected garment' (D E Hiebert, *1 Peter*, Moody, 1992, p 121).

Types: The list may be brief, but the implications are widespread. We are to remove the following: 'malice' (general New Testament word for depravity, 2.16); 'guile' (deceit, 2.22); 'hypocrisy' (duplicity, Matt 23.28); 'envies' (discontentment) and 'evil speaking' (defamation; the word is rendered 'backbiting' in 2 Corinthians 12.20).

Teaching: It should be noted that the particular errors to 'lay aside' relate to the areas of attitude and speech. If we allow these vices to take hold, then we fail to nurture spiritual growth and it will become evident to others.

TAKE IN!

Far from being empty, believers are to fill themselves with the word of God.

Description: Having just spoken on the 'new birth' (1.23), it is unsurprising that Peter then likens the believer to a 'newborn babe' (2.2). This is a vivid reminder to feed on that which develops spiritual health and energy – the word of God.

Diet: The 'milk' is further described as 'sincere' (pure) and 'spiritual' (see NIV rendering). As a child of God, I must feed on the word of God. A systematic and regular reading of the Bible will ensure that the diet is educational, varied and stimulating (Job 23.12; Psa 119.103; Jer 15.16).

Duty: The extent to which we feed on the word is a useful barometer to assess our spiritual health. Peter states that we are to 'desire' (or long for, Rom 1.11) the teachings of scripture.

Determination: Peter's ministry echoes the sentiment, 'Once bitten, forever smitten!' He states that having tasted (literally experienced) the goodness of Christ (Psa 34.8) we will long for more. How strong is our appetite for Christ? How often do we return for more?

Development: Although the context (and tone) is different, it is worth reading in parallel 1 Corinthians 3.1-2 and Hebrews 5.11-14. In summary, the word of God is our staple diet and all we need for spiritual progress.

GROW UP!

In avoiding sin (outlined in 2.1) and feeding on the scriptures and the Saviour (2.2-3), the believer is sure to grow in grace.

This growth will be

Virtuous: Peter states that we are to 'grow up in [our] salvation' (2.2, NIV). The reading of scripture is a virtuous circle for it develops our knowledge of salvation and the blessings we have in Christ – and that will inevitably impact on others.

Continuous: Christian growth does not happen overnight! As the apostle Peter himself would testify, there are inevitable ups and downs, but we need to keep going in our reading and study of the word.

Obvious: Others will be able to observe the growth, detecting those who spend time with God and His word (Acts 4.13).

Christ in you,

the *hope*

of *glory*.

Colossians 1:27

Study of a Book: Colossians

9

'The Epistle to the Colossians is a profound and priceless little document'

(J Sidlow Baxter, *Explore the Book*, Zondervan, 1966, Vol 6, p 202)

The study of scripture is a lifelong privilege and responsibility. In the context of the epistle to the Colossians, the following pointers may help us to 'rightly divide the word of truth' (2 Tim 2.15).

STUDY THE SETTING

Before tackling a book, it is worth standing back and asking a few questions. Who was used to write the book? Where was the writer based? What is the main purpose of the book?

Author: On this occasion, the writer is the apostle Paul (1.1,23; 4.18). Note references to his importance (1.1), intercessions (1.9), insight (1.25) and imprisonment (4.3,18).

Background: Colosse was located in Asia Minor (around 100 miles east of Ephesus). The area was rich in mineral deposits, but Paul points to a more abiding wealth in Christ (2.3). Opponents sought to peddle false teaching, denying the deity of Christ, promoting the worship of angels, and encouraging a return to Judaism. The epistle was written to counteract these errors.

Comparisons: The style and content of Colossians are similar to Ephesians (both were written around the same time, 4.7-8; Eph 6.21). As someone has said, 'In the Ephesians, the Church is the primary object, and the thought passes upward to Christ as the Head. In Colossians, Christ is the primary object, and the thought passes downward to the Church'.

SETTLE ON A STRUCTURE

Every book of scripture has its own internal structure. Three 'R's help unravel the divisions: **READ** (go through the book in one sitting); **RE-READ** (go through the book several times with different translations); **RESEARCH** (see what others think of the book and how it hangs together). With regard to Colossians, note

The Twofold Division: The four chapters of the epistle divide neatly into two: *doctrinal* (chapters 1–2), where the major theme is to present the foundations of the Christian faith, and *practical* (chapters 3-4), with an outline of the personal and corporate responsibilities of the believer. All activity in the Christian life must have a solid biblical foundation and we must also combine knowledge with action.

The Threefold Division: The epistle can also be divided into three. The first part (1.1-2.7) enables the reader to *discern Christ* – the unique and incomparable Saviour who is at the heart of the gospel. The second part (2.8-23) asks the reader to *defend Christ* –

particularly against other views that are contrary to scripture. The final part (3.1-4.18) equips the reader to *display Christ* – applying practical exhortations that help manifest the Saviour.

SCRUTINISE THE SECTIONS

Having grasped the overall structure, the next step is to dive into the detail. Using just one example (of many), consider how, in 3.1-17, the believer is exhorted to:

Put First: Our ambition should be to 'seek' that which is spiritual and eternal (3.1-4). Note the reference to 'seek' in Matthew 2.13, which indicates that this is not something casual or incidental. The present tense also indicates that this is something that the believer should do on a continual basis.

Put Off: Believers need to maintain holiness in their Christian lives (3.5-9). We are to discard immoral living as we would a stained garment, and live in a manner consistent with our profession of salvation.

Put On: The Christian is also called to display the 'new man' (3.10-14). The order of the various attributes mentioned in the passage is an indication that this is an 'inside out' transformation (vv 12-13), with love as the ultimate overcoat (v 14)!

Put Right: In an epistle emphasising the supremacy of Christ, the saints are to maintain happy fellowship by upholding the 'peace of Christ' (3.15, RV), the 'word of Christ' (3.16), and the 'name of Christ' (3.17).

SPOT THE SUBJECTS

Each book has particular themes, which the careful reader will seek to pinpoint and develop. Some examples are presented below which encourage us to be

Thankful: Almost the introductory words of the apostle are to express thankfulness (to God) for the saints at Colosse (1.3). An 'attitude of gratitude' remains an important characteristic of godly saints (3.15-17; 4.2).

Faithful: The apostle commends the saints at Colosse for their faithfulness (1.2). This was a general characteristic of the assembly, but it was also evident with certain brethren (1.7; 4.7,9). Faithfulness to God and His word is vital for all believers.

Prayerful: Developing a healthy prayer life is another subject central to the epistle, with Paul and his companions leading by example (1.3,9). Before concluding, the apostle exhorts his readers to adopt the same dependency upon God (4.2); in so doing, they will follow the example of Epaphras (4.12).

SEE THE SAVIOUR

Because the Lord Jesus is the central theme of scripture (Luke 24.27), readers must therefore 'look for the Lord' in their Bible study. In Colossians, the Lord can be located

In Person: The epistle includes one of the most important declarations on the deity of Christ (1.14-20). Note the exposition of His character and marvel at His uniqueness and love.

In Picture: False teachers sought a return to circumcision, but Paul was clear that Christians had already undergone a spiritual circumcision in Christ (2.11). Water baptism also pictures our burial and resurrection with Christ (2.12).

In Principle: To 'put on' the new man, with its associated attributes (3.12-14), is an exhortation to display Christ. For example, the opening to the section describes the believer as 'elect', 'holy' and 'beloved' (terms that can be applied to the Saviour: see Isaiah 42.1; Luke 1.35; 3.22).

In Precept: The apostle exhorts the saints to allow the 'word of Christ' to dwell within them (3.16). This refers to the teachings of Christ and the importance of allowing them to guide and influence our attitude and actions.

In People: Epaphras, a local saint who visited Paul (1.7-8; 4.12) is described as a 'servant of Christ'. These and other believers were men of God who displayed Christ (one even carried the name 'Jesus', but he used a second name to differentiate himself from the Lord, 4.11).

Colossians
'Treasures of Wisdom' (2.3)

Date: AD 60-62
Place of writing: Rome
Author: Paul   'apostle', 1.1
                 'a minister', 1.23
                 'remember my bonds', 4.3,18
Key verses: 1.15; 2.3; 3.1-2; 4.2
Compare/Contrast: Ephesians, Philemon

Key Words
'preeminent' (to be first): 1.18
'reconcile': 1.20,21
'cross': 1.20; 2.14
'increasing/increaseth': 1.10; 2.19
'knit together': 2.2,19
'are risen with': 2.12; 3.1
'put off': 3.9
'giving thanks': 1.3,12; 3.17
'pray': 1.3,9; 4.3
'faith': 1.4,23; 2.5,7,12

D O C T R I N A L	**Discerning Christ** *'Who is the image of the invisible God'* 1.15	**1.1-2**
		Introduction
		1.3-2.7
		1.3-8 Appreciation 1.9-13 Supplication 1.14-20 Exaltation 1.21-23 Reconciliation 1.24-29 Revelation 2.1-5 Education 2.6-7 Exhortation
	Defending Christ *'Let no man'* 2.16,18	**2.8-23**
		2.8-10 Let no man spoil you 2.11-17 Let no man judge you 2.18-19 Let no man beguile you 2.20-23 Let no man enslave you
P R A C T I C A L	**Displaying Christ** *'Put on ... mercies, kindness, humbleness of mind ...'* 3.12	**3.1-17**
		3.1-4 Something to put first 3.5-9 Something to put off 3.10-14 Something to put on 3.15-17 Something to put right
		3.18-4.17
		3.18-4.1 Private life 4.2-4 Prayer life 4.5-6 Public life 4.7-17 Personal life
		4.18
		Salutation

Daniel ... a

man greatly beloued

Daniel 10:19

Study of a Character: Daniel *10*

'Daniel: God's man in a secular society'

(Donald K Campbell, Discovery House, 1988)

One feature of the scriptures is that they contain a rich and varied collection of character studies. For the purposes of this study, let's consider Daniel.

CONTEXT

The starting point in studying a Bible personality is to consider the setting. For Daniel, note the following:

Historical: Daniel lived at a time of momentous change. God allowed a foreign force (Babylon) to take His Jewish people captive (1.1-2). Daniel therefore experienced the commencement of the 'times of the Gentiles' (Luke 21.24).

Spiritual: Moses had previously warned the nation of Israel that failure to obey God would bring certain judgment (Deut 28.15-68). This was fulfilled in Daniel's day as God's people returned to a position of slavery.

Cultural: As an inhabitant of Babylon, Daniel knew what it was to live 'away from home' (1.6). As with Joseph, he resisted the danger of conforming to the culture of his day (Gen 39.7-9; Dan 1.8). We too need to follow their example (Rom 12.1-2).

Occupational: Irrespective of the world power (Babylon, Medes and Persians), Daniel was elevated to various positions of importance (1.19; 2.48; 5.31–6.3). As Daniel himself testifies, the promotion came from above (1.17; Psa 75.6-7).

Doctrinal: Daniel is used to Jehovah being extolled as 'the Most High God' (for example, 3.26; 4.2,17; 5.18; 7.18). In addition, Daniel conveyed a unique prophecy – foretelling the exact time when Messiah would present Himself to the nation of Israel, face rejection, but ultimately provide eternal blessing (9.25-26).

CHRONOLOGY

Bible characters develop over time. It is therefore important to consider the character in sequence. Daniel lived through the entire period of captivity (1.21), lasting 70 years (Jer 25.11-14; 29.10-14). We are therefore able to glean truth from three distinct phases of his life.

Truth for the Teenager: In the opening chapter, Daniel and his friends are described as 'children' (1.4,17). The term is descriptive of young men who were able to live godly lives as teenagers.

Ministry for the Middle-Aged: At the end of his three-year course (1.5,18) Daniel entered into service in the royal court. History indicates that Nebuchadnezzar ruled for 40+ years, so Daniel must have been in his mid 50s during the incident recorded in chapter

5. Note the references in chapter 5 verses 11 and 12, and chapter 6 verse 23, and consider how Daniel remained true to God.

Encouragement for the Elderly: Growing older and colder is a sad feature of many Bible characters – but not Daniel! The captivity of Israel ended under the reign of Cyrus (10.1; Ezra 1), by which stage Daniel would be in his mid to late 80s. Despite his advanced years, Daniel remained sensitive to the plight of God's people – note his description in chapter 10 verse 19.

CHARACTER

But what made Daniel tick? The book that carries his name is full of insights. Consider, for example, his

Ancestry: Daniel came from a family background that was noble in character (1.3). The concluding chapters of 2 Kings present the Jews (both the nation and the royal family) as sinful, but Daniel was different. It is equally important for us to remain faithful irrespective of how others live.

Burden: Daniel was wholehearted in his commitment to please God and he sought to retain the distinction between himself and his captors (1.8-16). Is this what burdens the people of God today?

Courage: The song 'Dare to be a Daniel' is apt for he was happy to speak out for the truth (1.8; 2.16), no matter the personal cost (6.10). Men of principle are also men of power.

Dependency: Daniel was a man of prayer, and not just when he faced opposition – note the conclusion in chapter 6 verse 10. His dependency upon God can be viewed in terms of the frequency, posture, spirit, and content of his prayers (see also 9.4,20).

Education: As with Moses (Acts 7.22), Daniel was taught the ways of a foreign people, but the ultimate source of his 'knowledge' (reasoning skills and thought processes) was Jehovah (1.17). God remains the source of wisdom for believers today (James 1.5).

Faithfulness: We have already noted the chronological detail to Daniel's life, but notice the twofold reference to his 'heart' – at the beginning and end he remained faithful to Jehovah (1.8; 10.12). An apt summary of Daniel is found in chapter 6 verse 4. Hebrews 11.33 also refers to him.

Gift: During His earthy ministry, the Lord upheld the historicity of Daniel as a 'prophet' (Matt 24.15). His ability to decode dreams and point forward to Messiah was a divinely ordained gift. There are no prophets today, but God still gifts His people to serve Him (1 Cor 12).

COMPANIONS

Daniel was undoubtedly influenced by his friends, particularly given their own devotion to God (1.6,7,17,19,20; 3.12-30). In addition, scripture refers to Daniel in the same breath as Noah and Job (Ezek 14.14,20). The adage is true – 'You get like the company you keep!' We should therefore choose our friends carefully as they **will** influence our outlook as Christians.

CHALLENGES

In studying Bible characters, we should always seek to identify the key lessons and challenges for today. We can learn the following from Daniel:

Sovereignty: 'The theme of the book is the sovereign rule of God over the realm of man' (Renald E Showers, *The Most High God* –

A Commentary on the book of Daniel, The Friends of Israel Gospel Ministry, 1994, p xiv).   Note how this truth is established from the outset of the book (1.2,9,17).

Spirituality: Throughout his life Daniel was able to combine holiness and humility.   He displayed the character of God (4.18; 5.11) and acknowledged that his powers were sourced in heaven (2.30; 9.3-4).

Scriptures: If Daniel read and studied the scriptures (9.1-2), then we too must read them regularly and systematically.

Supplications: Prayer should be part and parcel of the Christian's daily routine (6.10).

Saviour: Daniel recorded some important insights into the person and work of Messiah (2.44-45; 7.9-14; 9.25-26).   Spirit-filled Bible characters will point our thoughts to the Saviour.

Let the

beauty

of the

Lord our *God*

be upon us.

Psalm 90:17

Study of a Psalm: Psalm 90 *11*

'The 90th Psalm might be cited as perhaps the most sublime of human compositions - the deepest in feeling - the loftiest in theological conception - the most magnificent in its imagery'

(C H Spurgeon, *The Treasury of David, Volume 2*, Hendrickson, p 67)

As the longest book in the Bible, one that we often resort to in times of adversity, it is worth considering how we might get to grips with a Psalm. Below are some general and specific points, using Psalm 90, that may help us in our study.

P - POSITION

The book of the Psalms belongs to the poetic part of the Old Testament and some contextual points should be noted.

Spiritual Songs: The word 'Psalm' signifies music accompanied by stringed instruments. The book is a collection of hymns for Israel to praise Jehovah (see Psalm 145). It is therefore limited in its teaching for believers today – for example, specific instruction on 'church truth' is absent.

Poetic Pentateuch: The book has a five-fold division which parallels the introductory books of the Bible. Psalm 90, for example, commences the fourth section. With an overall emphasis on wandering (as in the book of Numbers), it ends appropriately with Psalm 106. In studying individual Psalms, it is important to keep in mind their position relative to the overall book.

Human Hearts: The Psalms span a significant period of Israel's history. From Moses (Psalm 90) through to the kings and beyond, they reflect the innermost thoughts of Israel and their leaders. The Psalms are thus ideal material to help us prepare for worship and thanksgiving.

Messianic Ministry: We should remember that certain Psalms can only be interpreted in light of the Lord Jesus (Psalm 2,8,16, 22,24,40,41,45,68,69,72,89,91,102,110, and 118). 'The Messianic Psalms deserve sincere and serious study. They will richly repay and reward time spent in meditation upon them, for a study of these Psalms is nothing less than a study of Christ Himself' (J M Flanigan, *What the Bible Teaches – Psalms*, John Ritchie Ltd, 2001, p 16).

S - STRUCTURE

Individual Psalms have their own unique structure, and a suggested division of Psalm 90 is outlined below.

Man and his Maker (vv 1-6): Whereas the Lord is eternal (and Creator, v 2), man is mortal and part of creation (v 3). The section presents a sharp distinction between the timeless character of Jehovah (v 4) and the temporary abode of humans on earth (v 5).

Sin and its Sentence (vv 7-11): All sin is known to Jehovah (v 8) and brings certain judgment upon the perpetrators (vv 7,9-11). The time-bounded span of life was of relevance to the Israelites, particularly with the destruction of the older generation in the wilderness (Num 14.29-34).

Prayer and its Petition (vv 12-17): This section of the Psalm deals with the request of Moses for wisdom, joy, and fellowship with Jehovah.

A - AUTHOR

Aside from the divine Author (2 Tim 3.16), certain Psalms have an attributed human author (Moses in the case of Psalm 90). What then do we know of Moses from this Psalm?

Importance: Moses is described as the 'man of God' (Deut 33.1). This is a designation reserved for a select few in scripture and reflects the prophetic office held by Moses. The New Testament believer can grow into a state of spiritual maturity by following the instruction of scripture (1 Tim 6.11-12; 2 Tim 3.16-17).

Reverence: Moses begins and concludes his prayer by addressing Jehovah as 'Lord' (vv 1,17), which is a display of reverence. The believer today is privileged to know God as 'Father' (Matt 6.9), but, as with Moses, we need to be reverent as we address Him in prayer.

Eloquence: The man who was 'mighty in words' (Acts 7.22) was equally able to strike lofty notes of praise. In terms of worship, Moses is a good example for us to follow.

Intelligence: Moses knew that man is mortal (verse 3 translates a Hebrew word for 'man' which means frail or weak). The less we think of ourselves the better we are in the sight of God.

Persistence: The Psalm is not the only insight into the prayer life of Moses. Study of this Psalm should lead us to consider other incidents when the 'man of God' prayed (for example, Exodus 32.11-13; Numbers 14.13-19).

L - LORD

Each Psalm carries important instruction about Jehovah. For example, in Psalm 90 we learn the following:

Habitation: Moses spoke of the Lord as the refuge for His people (v 1). The Tabernacle has come and gone but the New Testament believer, who enjoys fellowship with his local assembly, is no less privileged (1 Tim 3.15).

Exaltation: The opening two verses of the Psalm are rich in their understanding of God. In a Psalm that unfolds the power of the Lord, consider how He is eternal (v 2) and therefore without comparison.

Satisfaction: Despite the judgment in the Psalm, Moses desired times when he would be satisfied with the Lord's loving-kindness (v 14). Has that been our experience today?

Manifestation: The prayer of Moses concludes with a sublime request – that the people of God would reflect the beauty of God (v 17). Do we manifest this divine character to others (2 Cor 4.11)?

M - MINISTRY

Each Psalm has its own specific line of teaching. Psalm 90 presents some basic principles to help improve our prayer life. For example, consider the following features:

Necessity: If Moses considered it vital to supplicate heaven, then the same holds for believers today. We should each echo the desire of the disciples in Luke 11.1 – 'Lord, teach us to pray'.

Spirituality: Notice the sequence in the prayer of Moses – it begins with praise (vv 1-11) before moving to petition (vv 12-17). A necessary element of prayer (including intercessory prayer) is praise and thanksgiving (Phil 4.6).

Humility: Moses lived under the all-seeing eye of Jehovah (v 8) and took the low place before Him (consider, for example, the similes Moses used for mankind in verses 5 and 6).

Specificity: Moses had a clear view of what he wanted for himself and the nation – each phrase between verse 12 and verse 17 contains a specific request.

Brevity: Not to limit the time we spend in the sanctuary, but this prayer of Moses takes around two minutes to read.

We

preach ...

Christ Jesus

the

Lord.

2 Corinthians 4:5

Study of a Sermon: Acts 2 *12*

*'This sermon has basically one theme:
Jesus is the Messiah and Lord'*

('Acts', Stanley D Toussaint in *The Bible Knowledge Commentary*
(New Testament), Victor Books, 1983, p 358)

APOSTLES

Each sermon has a human agent responsible for delivery (2 Cor 4.7).
In the example of the sermon delivered on the Day of Pentecost, the
initial focus is on the apostles. Consider their

Responsibility: The mandate for the sermon in Acts 2 is found in
chapter 1 verse 8. The apostles were to act as witnesses, initially at
home in Jerusalem and then beyond. We too have a responsibility
to tell others of the gospel (1 Pet 3.15), but the starting place remains
with those we know best (Mark 5.19-20).

Company: The apostles were a unique, unrepeatable band of
disciples (witnessing the Lord's resurrection, 1 Cor 9.1-2) but chapter

1 verse 14 presents an important principle – a plurality of servants (Luke 10.1). Fellowship with other Christians is a command, not an optional extra (2.42; Heb 10.25)!

Dependency: During the ten days between the ascension and the Day of Pentecost (compare chapter 1 verse 3 with the 50 days between the feasts of First-fruits and Pentecost, Lev 23.15-16) the apostles were found in prayer (Acts 1.14). This mark of dependency needs to characterise Christians in the 21st Century.

Vocabulary: The Day of Pentecost is inextricably linked to the descent of the Holy Spirit (John 7.39). The speech of the apostles (able to dialogue in foreign languages, 2.4-8) was under the direct influence of the Holy Spirit. Though a unique event, we too need to be empowered with the Holy Spirit in our service (1 Cor 2.3-4).

Harmony: Peter may have been the spokesman, but he operated in unity with his fellow apostles (2.14,32). The local assembly needs to approach enemy territory with a united force!

AUDIENCE

Each sermon will have an audience and it is particularly important to note relevant details concerning the background on the Day of Pentecost.

When? As the Passover and First-fruits were unrepeatable events, marking the Lord's death (1 Cor 5.7) and resurrection (1 Cor 15.23) respectively, so too was the Day of Pentecost. The day marks the commencement of the church age (predicted in Matthew 16.18).

Who? The audience was Jewish, either from direct descent or comprising individuals who had converted to Judaism (2.5,10). The references to Jesus of Nazareth as Messiah (2.22), David (2.29), and the house of Israel (2.36) display an important principle – preaching in a manner relevant to the audience!

Where? Pentecost was one of three feasts required by male Jews to attend at Jerusalem (Exo 34.18,22-23). The city was therefore busy and an ideal opportunity to advance the gospel. This pattern is repeated throughout the book – apostles visiting thriving cities/ports to spread the gospel (16.12; 17.16-17; 18.9-11; 19.1).

Why? The Day of Pentecost was reckoned to be the anniversary of the giving of the Law (Exo 19.1). The events in Acts 2 are therefore in marked contrast to the giving of the law – 3,000 were judged for their idolatry (Exo 32.28), but, under grace, a similar number were saved (Acts 2.41).

What? The auditors summarize what they have just heard as 'the wonderful works of God' (2.11). The narrative testifies to the events being divine (of God); demonstrable (works) and delightful (marked by wonder).

ADDRESS

The primary focus of Peter's sermon highlights that both the Spirit and the scriptures testify of the Saviour as Messiah. The quotation from Joel refers to the Day of the Lord with two precursors – the descent of the Spirit and unprecedented judgment. The former occurred at Pentecost, but the latter remains to be fulfilled; an event which will bring repentance to Israel and millennial glory for Christ.

APPROACH

Although the surroundings and content are unique, there are important stylistic points to observe from Peter's sermon that are relevant for today.

Verbal: Peter stood before his audience and 'lifted up his voice' (2.14). In other words, he made the necessary steps to be both seen and heard! Furthermore, notice that the message was just that – a sermon containing words with no acting or drama.

Logical: As Peter develops the message, notice the terms which indicate the evidence of a rational argument: 'for' (2.15,25,34) and 'therefore' (2.30,33,36). The gospel demands the application of the mind (Isa 1.18). It is incumbent on the preacher to outline its salient features in a reasoned and logical manner.

Scriptural: The sermon is Bible-based, with references to Joel (2.17-21) and the Psalms (2.25-28,34). We too are called to 'preach the word' (2 Tim 4.2) and to do so we need to read it, study it, and memorise it. Gospel preaching demands an understanding of the context and meaning of scripture.

Reverential: Peter gives God His rightful place in the sermon. The scriptures are His written word (2.17); the work of Calvary was accomplished under His sovereign will (2.23); the Lord was raised from the dead by His power (2.24); He will yet bring the enemies of the Lord to a position of subjection (2.34), and the Father declares His Son to be both Lord and Christ (2.36). The sermon was therefore 100% devoted to God and His Son – an example for us to follow.

Devotional: If the message originates from God then its centre is naturally Christ. Peter declares the pre-eminence of the Saviour: His humanity ('Jesus' who dwelt in 'Nazareth', 2.22); His deity (attested by His miracles, 2.22b); His agony ('crucified and slain', 2.23); His victory ('raised up', 2.24); His supremacy (greater than Israel's model king, 2.29-31); His glory ('exalted', 2.33) and authority (awaiting vindication, 2.34-35 but is now both Lord and Christ, 2.36).

AFTERMATH

The concluding verses (2.37-47) outline the impact of the sermon.

Conviction: The convicting work of the Spirit (John 16.8-11) was evident with the people in Jerusalem (2.37). From start to finish, salvation is of the Lord (Jonah 2.9; Acts 2.47).

Change: The conversions experienced in the chapter were genuine. Note the emphasis on repentance, which may be defined as an amendment with abhorrence of past sins.

Continuation: Faith appropriates salvation but, if genuine, it soon manifests itself in good works (James 2.26). The evidence remains a desire to continue in the things of God (Acts 2.42).

Jesus

... spake many things
unto them in

parables.

Matthew 13:1-3

Study of a Parable: Luke 19.11-27

13

'Beyond the human story lies a
theological truth and a spiritual lesson'

(John Phillips, *Bible Explorer's Guide*, Loizeaux, 1987, p 114)

As certain parts of the Gospels are devoted to parables, it is important to consider how best they can be studied. Some suggestions are presented below, with a particular reference to the parable of the pounds (Luke 19.11-27).

PURPOSE

During His earthly ministry, the Lord made a decisive move to present a large element of His teaching by means of parables (Matt 13.1-15). Why?

Meaning: 'Parables in Scripture are stories that illustrate truths by means of comparison. The phrase, "the kingdom of heaven is like" means that elements in the story run tangent to truths about the kingdom' (Roy E Beacham in *Dictionary of Premillennial Theology*; General Editor Mal Couch, Kregel, 1996, p 231).

Method: Parables were designed to reveal truth to the believer and conceal it from the unbeliever (Matt 13.11-15). Notice, however, that even the disciples required an explanation (v 36) of the parables. Bible study remains a spiritual exercise, and the Holy Spirit indwells us to shed light on scripture (John 16.13).

Message: Each parable has a particular message to convey. In Luke 19.11-27 the message is that the establishment of the Lord's kingdom, though initially delayed because of His rejection (v 11), would eventually take place (v 15).

Mystery: In Matthew 13.11 the Lord spoke of the 'mysteries of the kingdom of heaven'. Previously He offered the kingdom to Israel (Matt 3.2; 4.17) but, with His rejection (12.24), the mystery refers to a period of time elapsing between the Lord's death/resurrection and the establishment of the kingdom.

Memorability: Depending on the definition, there are over 30 parables. In presenting the truth in this format, the Lord ensured that His ministry was vivid, memorable, and understood by His own (Matt 13.51).

POSITION

It was only following the formal rejection of the Lord (and His rejection of the nation) that He taught more with parables. Consider:

The Judgment on Judaism: In teaching with parables, the Lord exposed and condemned the blindness of Israel. This is manifest in the Lord's use of Isaiah 6.9-10 (quoted in Matthew 13.13-15 to explain parables, but also in Mark 4.11-12; Luke 8.10; John 12.39-

40; Acts 28.25-27 where Israel's rejection of her King is evident).

The Doctrine for Disciples: The disciples were naturally keen to know when the Old Testament promises of the kingdom would be fulfilled (for example, Acts 1.6). The parables therefore spoke of a delay in the establishment of the kingdom – but the delay allows for Gentile blessing and the church age (Matt 16.18).

The Help from History: In Luke 19 the Lord journeyed through Jericho on His way to Jerusalem. The parable of travelling to a far country to receive the authority to rule (v 12) may be a reference to Archelaus (the son of Herod the Great) who travelled to Rome to receive his rights to rule (and his palace was built at Jericho).

PARTICIPANTS

Each parable contains a range of characters central to the narrative. Regarding the parable of the pounds, consider:

The Nobleman: This is an apt reference to the Lord (v 12) – the person from nobility departs to a far country (heaven, Acts 1.11) prior to the establishment of His kingdom (Matt 25.31).

The Servants: The ten servants in the parable (v 13) denote the faithful remnant belonging to the Lord prior to His return to earth (but also, by application, believers today). We have each a responsibility to obey the Lord and work for Him during His absence from earth.

The Citizens: The citizens mentioned in the parable represent the nation of Israel who, on the whole, rejected the Lord as Messiah (v 14; John 19.15). Despite Israel's privileges (Rom 9.4-5), this description is a sad indictment of their spiritual blindness.

PROPHECY

The correct interpretation of the parables will help the believer understand some basic prophetic issues.

The City: The headquarters for Messianic rule is Jerusalem (Luke 19.11). The Son of David (Matt 1.1) must reign in the city of David's rule (2 Sam 5.5; Zech 14.4).

The Kingdom: The 'kingdom of God' (Luke 19.11) refers to the rule of Messiah upon earth. It is a literal kingdom, predicted in the Old Testament, and will be established when the Messiah returns to earth (v 15).

The Subjects: The inhabitants of the kingdom are those who obey the words of Messiah and are given positions of responsibility (vv 17-19). In contrast, prior to the commencement of His rule on earth Messiah will judge those who rejected Him (v 27; Matt 25.11-12, 41).

PRINCIPLES

Every passage of scripture contains important lessons for the believer (2 Tim 3.16) and the parables are no different.

Opportunity: Unlike the parable of the talents (Matt 25.14-30), each servant was given the same amount (Luke 19.13). Remember that we each have the same opportunities to serve the Lord (such as access to the scriptures and the reality of the indwelling Holy Spirit).

Fidelity: Two of the ten servants were commended for being 'faithful' (vv 17,19). The instruction was to 'trade' with the 'pound' (approximately three months' wages), and some were obedient to the request of the nobleman. As stewards, we too are required to be faithful (1 Cor 4.1-2).

Solemnity: One servant wrapped his pound in a 'napkin' (a cloth for wiping perspiration from the face, v 20 – he was disinclined to engage in labour!). His description of the nobleman as 'austere' (rough/ harsh, v 21) reveals him as 'wicked' (v 22). If this servant truly believed that the nobleman was austere, he would, at the very least, have placed the pound in the bank to gain interest (v 23). As with Judas, it is possible to appear as a servant of the Lord but *not* possess salvation.

Responsibility: Faithfulness in service will bring added responsibility in the future (vv 17,19). Our service will also be reviewed (and rewarded) in a coming day, and hence we should be industrious in light of the judgment seat of Christ (for example, 1 Corinthians 3.10-15; 2 Corinthians 5.10).

Humility: Notice that the parable stresses that the pound(s) belonged to the nobleman (vv 13,16,18,20). We can only serve the Lord with what He gives us. This should remove any thoughts of pride or self-importance.

them

through thy **truth**:

thy Word

is **truth**.

John 17:17

Study of a Doctrine: Sanctification *14*

'Sanctification is the greatest work God is doing in the Christian life, the process through which He is making us more Christlike for our good and His glory'

(Henry W Holloman in *Understanding Christian Theology*, General Editors Charles R Swindoll and Roy B Zuck, Nelson, 2003, p 947)

DEFINITION

An obvious starting point for studying a subject such as sanctification is to determine what it means! Three 'R's' may help.

Reading: Even the casual reader of scripture will encounter the word sanctify (and its family relatives – sanctified/sanctification). With almost thirty references in the New Testament alone it is clear that we are dealing with an important Bible doctrine.

Research: Digging a little deeper, we find that the word has a simple meaning: 'to make holy' or to 'set apart' (for example, the Sabbath, Priests and Tabernacle were all consecrated for service in the Old Testament, Genesis 2.3; Exodus 29.1,43). Sanctification is synonymous with holiness and separation from evil.

Resources: Access to Bible dictionaries (for example, W E Vine), Concordances (for example, Strong) and commentaries on the study of words (for example, A T Robertson, *Word Pictures in the New Testament*) are invaluable. Consider the following remarks by W E Vine: 'sanctification is not an attainment, it is the state into which God, in grace, calls sinful men, and which they begin their course as Christians' (*Vine's Complete Expository Dictionary of Old and New Testament Words*, Nelson, 1996, p 546).

REPETITION

Important Bible doctrines have numerous references throughout scripture. Some principles, outlined below, can help develop our understanding of Bible doctrines.

First Mention: To 'sanctify' is mentioned throughout scripture, with the first New Testament reference in Matthew 6.9. There God's name is 'hallowed', indicating that He is sacred and holy. Given our faith in Christ as Saviour, we too are reckoned as holy (1 Cor 1.30).

Frequent Mention: The book of Hebrews says more about sanctification than any other New Testament book. For example, we learn of the relationship between the Lord (as the sanctifier) and His people (as those who are sanctified) – Hebrews 2.11. The book further develops the basis by which the people of God are set apart (Heb 10.10,14; 12.14; 13.12).

Final Mention: Interestingly, the final book (and chapter) of the New Testament makes reference to sanctification (Rev 22.11 –

rendered as holiness). The believer will be faithful to scripture (v 7), devoted to God (vv 8-9), and resolute in being holy/sanctified (v 11).

The Role of each Person of the Trinity in Sanctification		
Father	Son	Holy Spirit
Planned sanctification	Provided sanctification	Performs sanctification
Architect	Administrator	Applier
Ultimate Source of sanctification	Intermediate Agent in sanctification	Direct Agent in sanctification
1 Cor 8.6; Heb 10.10	1 Cor 1.30; 8.6; Eph 5.26; Heb 2.11; 10.10,14	1 Cor 6.11; 2 Thess 2.13

(Charles R Swindoll and Roy B Zuck, *Understanding Christian Theology*, Thomas Nelson Publishers 2003, p 958)

INVESTIGATION

An exciting element of Bible study is the ability to search out new truths. Exploring scripture requires interest, commitment, and focus. In terms of sanctification, consider the following:

Aspects: Sanctification is multi-dimensional, as illustrated in the tables. The Bible speaks of pre-conversion sanctification (2 Thess 2.13; 1 Pet 1.2): the Holy Spirit sets people apart to bring them to Christ; positional sanctification (1 Cor 1.2; 6.11; Heb 10.10): the Christian is termed a 'saint' (set apart) because we are 'in Christ'; progressive sanctification (1 Thess 4.3): the believer lives in an ungodly world and needs to secure victory over sin and become more Christlike; perfect sanctification (Eph 5.25-27; Col 1.22): when Christ comes, we will be fully and eternally like Him.

Agents: How is God able to sanctify a sinner? A variety of people/ means are used: the Saviour's death provides the basis (Heb 10.14); the Spirit has a pivotal role in bringing the sinner to salvation (John 16.7-11; 1 Pet 1.2) and thereafter to make us better reflect the Saviour (Rom 8.9,14-15,26,29); the scriptures are the primary role by which the Spirit sets us apart (John 17.17); and saints should work together to keep each other focused on that which is good (Heb 10.24).

Sanctify

ἁγιάζω (hagiazo)
to *make holy*, (ceremonially) *purify* or *consecrate*;
(mentally) to *venerate*:-hallow, be holy, sanctify

(J Strong, 'A Greek Dictionary of the New Testament' in
Interlinear Greek-English New Testament, Baker Book House, 1989, p 7)

Adversaries: Various obstacles work to prevent the believer pursue a sanctified/holy life (progressive sanctification). Various Old Testament characters provide some vivid examples: the power of Satan (Adam and Eve in Genesis 3); the temptation of the world (Joseph in Genesis 39) and the weakness of the flesh (David in 2 Samuel 11). We should, however, remember that this threefold opposition is met by a greater threefold power – each member of the Triune God is involved in the believer's sanctification.

Analogies: Again, in terms of progressive sanctification, the New Testament presents some striking illustrations to reinforce the importance of holy living for the believer. One example is found in Ephesians 4.22-24 and Colossians 3.8-14. As Christians, we are to live in a manner consistent with our profession by 'putting off' that which characterises the world and 'putting on' Christlikeness.

VARIATION

Bible doctrines can be compared with each other to note their different points of emphasis. For example, the table below draws some distinctions between justification and sanctification.

Justification	Sanctification
Deals with our standing	Deals (mostly) with our state
Declared righteous	Become righteous
What God does for us	What God does in us
Right relationship with God	Separation from sin
Makes us safe	Makes us sound
Legal perspective	Moral perspective

(Emery H Bancroft, *Elemental Theology,* Academie Books, 1977, p 285-6)

Three Types of Sanctification		
Positional Sanctification	**Progressive Sanctification**	**Perfective Sanctification**
Past point - Spiritual birth	Present process - Spiritual growth	Future point - Spiritual perfection
Salvation from the penalty of sin	Salvation from the power of sin	Salvation from the presence of sin
"I have been saved" (Eph 2.8-9)	"I am being saved" (James 1.21)	"I will be saved" (1 Thess 5.9)
Consecration of the body (1 Cor 6.19-20)	Deterioration of the body (2 Cor 4.16)	Redemption of the body (Rom 8.23)
Redemption of the soul commenced	Redemption of the soul continued	Redemption of the soul completed
Justification and regeneration	Sanctification	Glorification
Adoption as God's sons	Maturation as God's sons	Manifestation as God's sons
By the Father's will (James 1.18)	In the Father's world (John 17.17)	At the Father's time (Matt 24.36; Acts 1.6-7)
Through faith in Christ's work of crucifixion and resurrection for us (Acts 16.31; Rom 3.22-26)	Through Christ's present work of intercession for us and His power in and through us (Heb 7.25; Eph 3.17; Phil 4.13)	Through Christ's future return and transformation of us (Phil 3.20-21; 1 John 3.1-2)
Of and by the Spirit (John 3.5; Titus 3.5)	From the Spirit (2 Cor 3.18)	Through the Spirit (Rom 8.11)

(Charles R Swindoll and Roy B Zuck, *Understanding Christian Theology*, Thomas Nelson Publishers 2003, p 950)

APPLICATION

Of course, if Bible doctrines are to have any value then they must be applied. Below are some of the practical lessons we can glean from a study of sanctification.

Love for the Lord: The atoning work of the Saviour on the cross is foundational to each aspect of sanctification: it is the only basis for salvation (Heb 10.10), cleansing from ongoing defilement (1 John 1.7), and our future perfection (1 John 3.2). Study of a Bible doctrine such as sanctification ought to draw us closer to the Saviour and more earnest to worship Him.

Security of the Saint: The saints at Corinth were far from practising holy living (1 Cor 5). However, despite their practices the believers at Corinth are still classified as 'saints' (1 Cor 1.2). Rejoice in the truth of eternal security (John 10.28) but remember it does not provide us with a licence to sin (Rom 6.1-2).

Blessing from the Bible: The Saviour stressed the role of the word of God to enable the believer to pursue a sanctified life (John 17.17). Hence we have a fitting end to a series on the Bible – only by the daily and conscientious reading of scripture can we become more like its theme: the Saviour.

Graeme always had an interest in encouraging young people to study and enjoy their Bible. Back in 1996, when invited to speak to a group of young people, he used the opportunity to introduce them to various techniques on studying the Bible using helpful aids. He took Acts 12 as an example, suggesting possible approaches and identifying suitable resources. This appendix details the accompanying notes he provided for the group.

It is hoped that this appendix will prompt the reader to a greater in-depth approach to Bible study. It is far from an exhaustive study of Acts 12, but just provided a few useful pointers in the 45 minutes Graeme had with the group. It was intended to whet the appetite and illustrate the usefulness of dictionaries and concordances to enhance Bible study. Of course, since this was originally written, the world of technology has advanced and Graeme would doubtless recommend the e-Sword online Bible, which he used frequently. It takes the pain out of concordance and Strong's number searching, with the added advantage of being free!

Appendix

'You see everything Mr Holmes.'
'I see no more than you,
but I have trained myself
to notice what I see.'

(Sherlock Holmes, *The Adventure of the Blanched Soldier*)

The ultimate goal when studying the Bible is to learn more about the One that it reveals – the Lord Jesus Christ. He is the golden thread that runs throughout the scriptures (Luke 24.27). The history of the Bible is the history of two men: Adam and the Lord Jesus. However, the one important aim is to 'look for Him' as we employ various techniques to study the scriptures.

Acts 12 is a good chapter to answer the question 'How should we study the Bible?' We will use it to determine some approaches to Bible study. Consider the importance of:

THE SETTING

Whether studying a book, chapter or verse in the Bible, one of the most important starting points is to consider where it is placed in relation to what follows, and what has gone before.

In other words, why does the book of Acts follow directly from the Gospels? Chapter 12 starts with the words 'Now about that time...'. This means that we have to read the preceding chapters to determine the context (read chapter 11 verses 21-24).

Verses 3 and 4 of chapter 12 are also helpful in determining the context. 'Days of unleavened bread', 'Easter', and 'Passover'- why would this period be charged with violence towards the Christian?

THE SUBJECT(S)

Regarding the book, chapter or verse being studied, two questions to ask are:

> (1) What are the key events?
> (2) Who are the key people?

For example, the key event in Acts 12 is the imprisonment of the apostle Peter. Here we can use Strong's concordance, which will indicate how often the word 'prison' occurs. It will also show if there is any significant pattern, and help to identify other key Bible characters that were put in prison.

The concordance also tells us that the word 'prison' occurs on 21 occasions in the book of the Acts. An interesting pattern emerges from 19 of these references:

6 times in chapter 5 (vv 18,19,21,22,23,25)
5 times in chapter 12 (vv 4,5,6,7,17) and
8 times in chapter 16 (vv 23,24,26,27(twice),36,37,40)

Therefore, through using the concordance we can observe that in the book of Acts, there are THREE ESCAPE FROM PRISON STORIES!

Chapter 5   - the angel releasing the twelve apostles
Chapter 12 - the angel releasing Peter and
Chapter 16 - the earthquake opening the doors of the prison
              and undoing the chains of Paul and Silas

Also, by using the concordance we can determine the first character in the Bible, Joseph, who was put in prison (Gen 39.20). The law of first mention can be used to identify interesting features that can be traced throughout the Bible.

The key people of the book or chapter are relatively easy to identify. For example, the key man in Acts chapters 1 to 12 is Peter. In Acts chapters 13 to 28 the key man is Paul. In Acts 12, other key people in the chapter include Herod and Rhoda.

Character studies are very rewarding - look for their personalities, the places where they came from and the impact they have.

For example, in the case of Peter it is important to identify the key events in his life. John 1 records his calling as an apostle, and the importance of the name change that the Lord gave him in verse 42. The two occasions where he was given an object lesson on fishing are recorded in Luke 5 and John 21. A memorable moment in the life of Peter was his denial of the Lord in Luke 22. Additionally, especially with the apostles, it is vital to read their writings, in this case 1 and 2 Peter. Often they expound on the spiritual significance of their experiences with the Lord Jesus.

Regarding the character Herod, it is helpful to identify him in the historical context as Herod Agrippa I. He was the nephew of the Herod that murdered John the Baptist, and the one who interviewed the Lord Jesus before Calvary. He was also the grandson of Herod the Great - in whose reign the Lord was born. A good Bible dictionary is essential for learning more. For example:

1 'The Pictorial Encyclopedia of the Bible', published by Regency/Zondervan Press
2 'A Concise Bible Dictionary' by George Morrish, published by Chapter Two
3 'Fausset's Bible Dictionary' by Andrew R Fausset, published by Zondervan

THE SECTIONS

When studying a book or chapter, it is helpful and important to separate the writings into sections. These sections may embrace a key portion of teaching or perhaps just a key word.

Most Bibles give their own sections, such as Newberry, Scofield or Ryrie. However, a useful two volume set of books for this section study is *Jensen's Survey of the Old and New Testament* published by Moody Press.

Once you have identified the key sections, the next stage is to summarise them by either a word or phrase.

For example, in the case of the book of Acts, the period of approximately thirty-eight years can be sub-divided into two sections:

> Ch 1 - Ch 12.....Work around Jerusalem, Judea and Samaria
> Ch 13 - Ch 28...Work going out to the rest of the world

In the case of Acts 12, the chapter can be sub-divided into three sections:

> Acts 12.1-5.........Persecution of the church
> Acts 12.6-19.......Prison experience of Peter
> Acts 12.20-25.....Punishment of Herod

THE SUBSTANCE

Perhaps the most fertile area of Bible study comes when we get down to considering the key verses of the chapter or key words of the verse. There are a number of books that are essential such as:

1   'Interlinear Greek-English New Testament' by George Ricker Berry, published by Baker Book House
2   'The Englishman's Greek Concordance' by George V Wigram, published by Baker Book House
3   'Vine's Complete Expository Dictionary of Old and New Testament Words' by W E Vine, published by Thomas Nelson Publishers

Note that each of these books must be numerically coded to Strong's Exhaustive Concordance.

This is when we become our own 'Sherlock Holmes', by training ourselves to notice what we see.   In Acts 12 we can apply this approach in two directions – by considering a key verse such as verse 5, and by examining certain key words.

In verse 5 of Acts 12 there are 19 words, and yet almost each one of them is conveying some truth.   For example, whilst we are being informed that the church was praying for Peter, we can identify certain items that characterised their prayers: